MW01275138

1

Twelve Loving Weeks

by

Rand Regier

Contents

Love, the most beautiful part of our marriage. We said it often, felt it in our embrace, and it shielded us from a world intent on challenging our bond. I'll be forever grateful we had this gift, and I wish it for you all.

-Rand

Preface

April 8, 2022

Today my precious wife Melanie was told she has twelve weeks to live on this earth. I am a believer in miracles and my prayer for her healing continues although I must face reality and medical fact. I struggle with despair knowing that 47 years is hardly the length of a full and fruitful life.

Her last chemo round weakened her bowel creating a perforation and an infection that has been going on for five months. They stopped treating it two weeks ago since many variations of antibiotics, derived from her own blood cultures, proved ineffective. Hope for a healing is fading, divine sutures closing off the free flow of poison between her organs are now an unarrived fact.

This wonder woman has now endured five major surgeries. Kidney, colon (twice), lung and brain. She amazes me every day, but this news has devastated us both. Lately she bubbles over in tears more than I have ever seen.

Our lives changed forever in a moment. Faced with losing her this soon has a finality for which I was not ready.

The last three years should have prepared us for this, but we always had a thread of hope provided by a courageous doctor and new medical techniques.

Who could possibly brace for an end, given any amount of time. Fairness and reason are now pointless and unproductive thoughts, even though my mind recklessly travels there.

I began writing on Facebook "Twelve Loving Weeks" to provide updates and hopefully good news. I was encouraged greatly by friends and family during my time of need. Your comments, likes, hugs and hearts were anticipated daily. It's notable how social media has turned out to be such a source for comfort in our modern society. Shortly after I began, I discovered creative writing. A new artform, words relayed to virtual canvas using the imagination of the reader.

This has also been a type of therapy giving me strength to press on. I also felt a need to simply document and remember this precious time I have been given with my bride of nearly thirty years. I never thought I'd be publishing anything like this. You, her friends, family and strangers, are part of a unique group, privileged to have shared the wonder that is Mel.

Chapter 1

Empty Nest

April 11

Our first night here together finally happened as I sat in the living room of our newly rented apartment, lights dimmed, listening to her breathing in perfect rhythm through the cracked doorway to our bedroom.

I had spent two weeks moving in, setting up all the necessary elements guided by Mel from her hospital bed, texts and screenshots flowing the effort. She was to be released from palliative care after months of care, well enough to go home but knowing she wasn't long for this earth.

I now have many quiet moments like this where I must face my own reality and prepare for what the future may be like. I love taking care of her, every part of it, and it's automatic at this point. A desperate action to function solely for her needs. I can't imagine doing anything else.

When she sleeps, I'm thankful she can escape her reality, it must be exhausting for her, every waking moment facing her tremulous end. Her fear of pain dominant in every breath, the drugs, artfully designed to redirect her symptoms, but only reaching so far needing constant adjustment. I only hope she's dreaming of something wonderful in contrast to the reality we've been witness to.

We had both thought about this day. Although we adore our kids, now in their twenties, we were ready to yield our house to them becoming their landlords. We were curious, how it might feel to just be "us" in a simple dwelling after three decades of a busy home. Four kids, the excitement, laughter, and endless love seemed impossible to detach from, but now it's time to slow the pace and focus on our special union, where it all began.

Mel spent hours in the hospital picking out the bright red counter appliances matching the Asian inspired black and red ceramic dishware, only a splash of her creative juices. She searched for plush modern furniture mixed with some of the lasting pieces we brought from home. It turned out to be quite a design statement and her first walk through was a prideful moment.

Months ago, she had mastered a game on her phone challenging her to compete with other room designers to create the winning ensemble rewarding her with a win over her competitors often and despise for the ones she lost. "They wouldn't know design if it bit their ass" she'd say wrinkling her brow. I'd smile remembering her adapted skills from our furniture store days, always dazzling the shoppers with her solutions.

She's always been a quick thinker, able to read gestures and mannerisms. A true people person, making friends in any situation. Now, the game on her phone sits dormant, she is satisfied winning the live version, only to be judged and relished by her, and me.

I lean back in the overstuffed chaise lounge closing my eyes remembering the last time we had an empty nest. That one hadn't been used yet. I breath a long sigh as my mind drifts to a young couple, newlyweds, her peeking from behind a pine branch heavy with a fluff of powdery snow, back indoors, a purple jumpsuit, her very pregnant as she placed ornaments on the Christmas tree. Our first home was a basement suite my uncle had rented us. Modest, dated but *our* humble beginning. Now I look around at our new apartment and realize the regression to simple again. "This is good" I think to myself, as I pray once more, God make it last.

In the morning I'll give her a cocktail of prescription drugs, then three more times during the day. She takes one for anxiety but others to mask the pain she would have and was dodging for the last five months. The oncologist remarked that the team in palliative care had become quite skilled in making custom drug plans to help cancer patients through their final painful months. They would have moved her directly to hospice otherwise.

The nights are usually from 9pm to 2am with an interruption to empty bodily fluids from her catheter and ileostomy pouch. This is a good thing as it shows she is functioning. If either of these stop it can turn serious. If drugs cannot correct them, it's a trip to the hospital. She discovered early on a simple can of coke is the best remedy for a blockage and has prevented many crisis scenarios.

She usually falls back asleep, and I lay awake. Sometimes I can sleep more but usually I am up for the day. Coffee has become my friend.

In the morning I'll prepare her avocado on sourdough toast with scrambled eggs, orange juice and a coffee which she usually has only one shallow sip. Her meds make her anxious and the width around the island in our kitchen is just wide enough for her to guide her walker around a few times until her courage announces, "we should walk the hallway," usually turning into a car ride and sightseeing.

Chapter 2

Fly Girl

April 12

Ours is a love story like you see in movies. We never strayed, always had healthy communication and fights were mere disagreements that were quickly resolved. I always felt a warm calm when she would call me at work from home or a beach somewhere when she was "working."

We always part with "I Love You" even if I'm running an errand, she taught me this early on when we were dating so long ago. She isn't the same bubbly self due to the many drugs she needs but she is mostly pain free, and I thank God for that.

We, like many couples would make a strong effort to always plan a date night, take time for us and the continued construction of what we have and what we want our future to be like. Often on date night, we would find ourselves in a restaurant just sitting silent, not awkward, just content to be in each other's presence. Our hands would find each other, smiles to follow and her lips mouthing those sweet words over the candlelight. Servers blush on approach but valued what they were witness to.

A small metal badge with "Melanie" engraved, fitted with a tiny palm tree insert was the subject of a frantic search we did many times before embarking on a trip to Vancouver Airport. She was well versed on the many dress requirements preventing a wright-up while trying to simply do her job. The dreaded badge was also a sore spot giving her name to unruly guests and their chance at grievance. So she did her best to hang her scarf in just the right way to cover it when necessary.

She was a flight attendant for an airline that was originally based out of Abbotsford BC. The way the airline began was unique. The founder, trying to avoid commercial costs, placed an ad in a newspaper asking for anyone wanting to fly to Calgary to contact him and split the weekly bill of a private charter, the rest was an organic birth of one of Canada's leading airlines.

She was proud of her job often taking pictures of the runway sunrise, wingtips in the foreground, but in my mind, I would prefer seeing the warm smile on the other side, imagining it now as I write.

Her love for this job was unlike others she had over the years, this one involving lasting friendships and warm destinations sometimes bringing me for only one day of sand and warmth, but we were together, not to mention the special treatment of her working the isle, stealthily dropping treats on my lap, who wouldn't love that.

Today her hope of flying is gone even for pleasure, we're content just to be together. If you were to visit, you would notice she is closest to being herself in the middle of the day. We met with our new doctor yesterday and he said "she doesn't look like a person that has a few weeks to live rather think about longer and plan some short-day trips. Enjoy friends while she's mobile and feeling good."

She is still Mel and moments in the day can remind us of her quick wit and comments that always make us laugh. From 6pm until bedtime at 9, her tiredness is apparent, and her anxiety begins. There are times of clarity when I am on my knees tending to her, and I'll be startled by her fingers stroking my hair, "thank you for caring for me" she says. I stand and we embrace, all feels good again as I pray again "God please suspend this moment."

Last night I was woken three times to find her wandering about, simply confused at times, or needing pills for nausea and indigestion. Cabbage rolls, perogies & sausage was not the best plan, but she did enjoy a great Mennonite meal while visiting with our daughter Savannah and I am so glad she has her appetite, food right now, in any form, is energy.

April 14

A teary 2 am this morning she was sitting up standing sitting again half asleep but aware she needed something. I go to the kitchen returning with the meds she needs to continue her sleep and I hold her util she's once again in that perfect rhythm of ZZ's.

She needs me more than ever. I hesitate to leave her alone in the apartment and usually she's happy to wait in the car while I hunt for specific items at the grocery store or the pharmacy. I can't imagine what's going on in her mind when considering her predicted fate. The afterlife isn't something we talk about, but it must be weighing heavy in her thoughts. I'm honored to do anything for her, if I can figure out what that is on an hourly basis.

I'm her life-size teddy bear, the one person she can hold tightly for as long as she needs. When I hold her, it takes me back to one of our first dates coming back from Vancouver, her stretched over the console, head on my shoulder. She said something masked by the drone of the engine. I knew what she said but I needed to hear it for sure. What was that babe? I didn't hear you. "Oh, nothing," She wouldn't give it to me again that night, but I knew she said it for the first time. "Melanie, I love you back" I said out loud followed by her clutch tightening on my arm.

I miss so many parts of her that have fallen away. She's bound to a rolling walker, so we no longer hold hands in hallways. We tried a walk at Mill Lake, but she made it thirty feet and relinquished to her limit, so we turned back. The look given from strangers on the path was of sadness and empathy, first at her then me. I'm thankful we can still hold hands while driving. I also thank God for her sweetness. With brain surgery it could have been mood swings or anger which she deserved, frustration for cards dealt, but she keeps true to her form, always positive, always a smile reserved for me at any moment.

Chapter 3

Mel and Books

April 18

She can't bring herself to form a text let alone write paragraphs and posts. Books were always her escape, but it's been months since she's read one. She tries and usually can't read more than a few sentences, but she'll carry her favorite read around from the couch to the kitchen then her nightstand. I'm hoping it's due to the drugs and steroids, and not associated to her brain surgery and radiation. They said she'll have swelling for about two months, they have her scheduled for a follow-up phone interview May 18th.

Mel is a strong reader. Speed reading faster than I've ever seen, enabling her to breeze through a thick novel in a day and work materials or union agreements retaining all the key points. Pilots and co-workers frequently contacted her for such needs, she complied even through her medical challenges. I'm glad she could help others, it did give her a distraction, an extra connection to friends and her job, I'm sure also a sense of normalcy.

Her abilities are limited now, if you're wondering, she does see your messages but can't focus too long. Know that she would respond. It would be sweet and well worded. Know that she loves you.

April 22

Cultus Daytrip

Yesterday we ventured out to Cultus Lake just for the drive mainly. When we got to a very empty parking lot at the beach, she was sure there was a bear on the shoreline. I remarked the stump had a unique shape that might look like a bear, but she was adamant she would not be getting out of the car.

She's been seeing cats in our suite and dark clumps of dirt in the distance are assumed to be dogs. I was hoping that the hallucinations are merely the side effects of the drugs, but the doctor now wants an MRI. I really hope it's not any type of brain swelling or more tumors. She's already at a maximum dose of steroids and I'm not sure if there's more they can do.

Her days are very foggy, and she's lost her mid-day clarity I had looked forward to lately. I keep a close eye on her, put the stove on lock, clean butter out of the scissors and other odd discoveries if I don't.

I am hoping they can sort out what she needs, and we can get her back again. She is here all day, but I miss her very much.

Chapter 4

April 23

Pain, Divine Comfort

Hard choice yesterday was to listen to Mel's request and go to the ER and hope for a pleasant experience but we both knew she needed back into palliative care and everything channels through the exhausted emergency entrance. Any ER lately is a gong show and the staff are doing their best. There simply are not enough beds and too many patients who really don't need to be there. Luckily, the admissions clerk recognized her situation and got her a temporary bed after we had only waited an hour or so.

Going through proper channels for her prescriptions is now complicated. The Doctor here must do his own assessment even though palliative care had established her specific needs and drugs that would keep her pain free. She needed morning meds which I had along in her knapsack, but rules stated that I had to wait for them to do their process and order the same meds from their drawers. Morning meds I usually gave her at 8am were finally administered at 1pm, This meant a period of pain but confirmation that her regiment for the last two months was necessary and accurate. During the night they had put restraints on her to limit the harm she was doing to herself, she had pulled out her catheter, the traces of blood stains near her fresh bed sheets told the story for me, I was so saddened she had gone through the torment while I went home exhausted, trying to get a minimum amount of sleep. In hindsight, I should have just maintained her drug schedule defying their protocol. I could have saved her that horrible night and morning.

She's sedated now and comfortable but still in the restraints. I took liberty to untie her while I could sit with her. A little bright spot came when I was helping her sit up hanging her legs off the side of the bed. She was so relieved, she thanked me immensely saying it felt so good.

She sat there for a few minutes and suddenly smiled large. I asked her what made her smile and she said "Grandpa." Which Grandpa? "Wiebe" she said. I don't know what made her think of him, but he was my grandpa on my mom's side who we spent much time with when the kids were small. On his death bed he managed to play ball with Austin, three at the time, Henry hung his hand over the side and Austin repeated putting the ball in his hand, he would flatten his fingers to allow the ball to drop and roll to him on the floor. In his pain he found a way to give enjoyment to Austin and us all. I genuinely believe she got some comfort today from him, either from her memory or his spirit was there. I asked her to give him a big hug, for what it was worth, I still miss him dearly.

The next few days or weeks will most likely be spent here in Abby Hospital, but hospice is most likely soon. Her CT scan shows progression of her brain tumors, and it is causing the delirium and anxiousness. I can still hope for some moments of clarity, but it doesn't seem likely. I know some of you would like to visit and I don't want to restrict you, but it may be best to remember her laughter and her wit from your various times with her. She and I love you all and are thankful for you being a part of her life and her journey these last three years.

Chapter 5

Battle Scars

April 24

Walking to my car tonight from the ER I realized I'll never sell it. The bright colored yellow bumblebee was what she bought me after the silver one was totaled, with her behind the wheel. That car, and some angels, saved her from a fatality in 2016 giving me six more years of her in my life.

The Accident

1:00 am I was woken with a call from Mel, panicked. "Rand, I wrecked your car, and I can't get out" her voice quivering. She was on her way home from Vancouver airport after a late night at work. I usually picked her up, but it wasn't always possible, and she tried to be independent knowing it robbed me of my sleep and my own need to function at work.

"Where are you" I said. "Highway #1 after the Clearbrook exit but the front of your car is wrapped around a tree" she sobbed. "Are you ok, that's all that matters" I responded, adding "I'm on my way just stay on the phone." I put the cell in the cradle talking to her as I drove, trying to gain my senses from a dead sleep "what if I'm dreaming, no this is real, too real."

I arrived at the edge the highway, I could see headlights still on, the car's mangled nose and hood buckled high enveloping the tree. The engine had protected her and there she was climbing up the gentle slope in her uniform and heels, pulling her suitcase through the mud.

"Carry her bags"! the fire chief called out to the fireman beside her. "Yaa hero," Mel piped in "do your job!

My whole being exhaled, and I chuckled to myself, "my sassy girl was just fine" and so was I. The accident she explained was caused by a negligent truck driver who wouldn't let her change lanes to allow a car to merge from her right side. This combined with heavy rainfall, caused the car to lose control hydroplaning off the road. This Camaro I "liked" was now an unretrievable twisted mess, but I didn't care, she was safe.

1996; Mel & Rand, young family with two little blondies I kept entertained in the small Chevy Spectrum while waiting in front of the bank. Mel told me there was a surprise for me, moments later she returns with rent & bills money in hand.

"I'm confused" I said, "where did that come from"? Her reply "Well... remember how you had to sell your white sports car a few years back? I've had a Camaro fund going ever since but I'll have to start over."

I melted. My young wife, working in a daycare at the time, was squirreling away her hard-earned money so I could have a car I "liked"? She always kept others in mind like that. Never went out shopping for herself, hates shopping unless she was buying for someone else. I didn't care about selling that old car when I had those two gems in the back seat and that beauty at my side.

April 24

Summer 2019 Jazz fest New Orleans was an Important meetup for me especially because I had recently reconnected with a friend from 30 years ago. A college bud who was close like a brother. Mel didn't know Mike, or his sweeter side "Julia" very well but typically meshed the friendship quickly. The three-day event involved much walking, rewarded with Fogarty, Stapleton, and Widespread Panic. One day it had rained and was very muddy. I noted how the weather change was embraced by the fans, boys were prepared with rubber boots, the girls, colorful ones with flowers like you would expect for Nola and the "Woodstock" themed event.

All the walking and uneven terrain revealed a sprained ankle Mel thought was just a twist, but she pressed on not wanting to slow down the fun. She paid for it by being laid up for days after returning home. She is my Wonder Woman and always has been.

Caring for her has been a stark reminder of all she endured the last three years, changing her dressings and her clothes, helping her into the bath reveals all the battle scars her body wears proudly like medals of honor. So many surgeries and all the pain associated. Many times, she has had more than three tubes at once flowing meds in or poisons out and she never said "enough." We're all amazed and have commented at the "fighter" she is, but we didn't know all she was being subjected to and we didn't feel the shockwaves ripping through her body so many times. She brought four beautiful babies into this world, the pain and suffering of childbirth didn't come close. Women are acknowledged as having a higher pain tolerance, and I'm witness to that fact.

Looking at the full journey, I can understand but cannot believe she chose to go through everything she did without hesitance. She said once or twice, "I understand why some people just give up saying no more." Her reason was love and devotion. Hers for me, for our kids, family and of course the outreaching love for you, her friends.

On the medical side she is back in palliative care and out of the ER. The care she'll receive here is excellent in comparison, not to defame the ER staff since I know they have a hard daily road with many complexities.

Mel was already feeling the effects of the advanced treatments within an hour and their goal was to get her to a point where she wouldn't need restraints and she would have "calm" once more.

The doctor was noting her calcium has shot up and that could be contributing to her stress levels. That along with the refined drug regiment may give us more of our Mel back for the next bit. Let us hope and pray as you are faithfully doing already. I really appreciate you all!

Chapter 6

Crazy Magnet

April 26

I stayed the night with her since she was scared by a mouse in her dream last night. When I said I would stay she was thanking God. Her needing me is something I so appreciate, I regret if I ever took that for granted, although I rarely did since she was good at reminding me.

Thinking back to her pre-flight attendant days, we had every night together since the kids were little, since we were newlyweds. That new job was a problem I had to learn to deal with. I remember thinking hmm, I only get a fraction of the month with her now. Close to half of every year I was a single digit. I know she missed me too and called every night. It took about a year to come to terms with this new reality, but it never sat well with me.

If you know her closely you know what an involved conversationalist she is. She sure can tell a story, she has plenty and there's always laughter, always.

31

Another side thought is her ability to listen and help with her words. She would often tell me how she had talked with her coworkers about their life challenges, whether it was coming out and how their parents reacted, or family drug problems, or their own. She would be a comforting ear for so many, It's her gift. I probably won't know all the hearts she's helped over the years. Even in her younger days her co-workers were compelled to confide in her sharing their deepest thoughts and personal strife's. They even said, "I don't know why I'm telling you this", like she had given them some type of truth serum. I guess she was simply easy to feel comfortable around, and her advice was usually spot on.

If you're close, you'll also know she attracts crazy. Some of you know right away what I mean. Strange things happen around her, usually at high altitudes and once handled with a stern "mom look" which she did well, she would have a jewel of a story.

Today we'll wait for more clear moments as she sleeps and wakes or if there's a random comment when we thought she was sleeping while family carries on with bedside conversation. I pray she isn't scared when she wakes. It's been concerning me when she has been lately. At times, her body shivers and trembles. Please Jesus comfort her when I can't.

April 27

Chase, our youngest at 22 years and his Mama, these two share a very close bond not only because he was the "new baby" as little Austin said it back then, pointing to Colby as the "old baby." Mel is an excellent mother to all our kids and loves each of them dearly but these two went through a special hardship fifteen years ago when Chase was seven.

April 2007; A routine trip to the hospital in Regina turned into Chase being admitted to intensive care and a mystery disease. The doctors thought it may have been a flesh-eating type but couldn't slow it down. Mel couldn't leave his side and spent a series of weeks curled up beside him in a makeshift bed. Chase's prognosis was grim, and the nurses were preparing us, saying we may not want to go far from him for the weekend because his organs were probably going to start shutting down.

We had just gone through the horrific procedure of having a pic line inserted into our little boy's shoulder leading to his heart when a different doctor walked by. This doctor (sometimes I'm convinced he was an angel) picked up his chart and quickly deducted "strep in the bloodstream." He had seen it before in South Africa and said it was quite common there.

A quick switch of antibiotics and our precious Chase was home in a few weeks. Many prayer chains were activated across the country which I believe arranged that doctor to randomly appear.

Yesterday another crisis rifled through our family when Chase was again rushed to the hospital. He had passed out while having a coughing fit and thank goodness Aimee, his girlfriend, called an ambulance right away. Tests revealed he has pneumonia and fluid around his heart, but also a mass in his lungs which they biopsied right away. We may know the results today or tomorrow. Please pray for our boy.

My posts may be shorter, I'm sure you'll understand but I'll continue to keep things updated best I can.

Chapter 7

Shy Mel

April 28

We should get word about Chase's diagnosis today, we're all waiting, holding our breath. The prospect of having a whole new battle is just too hard to look at right now, but I do know I will fight with a vengeance for my beautiful son.

He's still in the hospital and now in a private room getting exceptional care and watching lots of movies. He isn't in pain and to talk with him and see him he seems perfectly well. For now, we'll wait on the doctors.

We all agreed not to talk about Chase when in Mel's room even though she was mostly sleeping now, I can't fathom the chance that she might hear something that would add stress in her fragile still state.

Lying here beside her, I think about what I miss the most, that would be her voice. I know that's cliche, but this is different. She could be inches away or calling me at work during a hectic day and her voice just saying hello the way she did brought a calming warmth that would deflate all the mind-clutter my head was in. Soon she would have all my problems solved, reciting a list of Thai appies and the green curry bowl she loved from her favorite restaurant in Blaine.

When we were young in our marriage she was shy, still hadn't come out of her shell. Hard to imagine I know. She was reluctant to talk to people and preferred to sink into a book for hours. She had a softer voice, young sounding, and when calls came in, they would ask to speak to her mom. I'm sure it made her feel self-conscious, and she was quite an introvert, always wanting me to deal with the outside world.

I was the one that talked to the neighbors and struck up conversations with random people in line-ups and gatherings, but when she got her first serving job at the Greek Restaurant "The Odyssey" it was busy, and she was forced to overcome her insecurities, becoming skilled at talking to strangers. I know, all your eyebrows are raised right? Mel, afraid to talk?

She never looked back. Her tips soared and so did her confidence. A few years later we had a fancy modern furniture store and she showed that her people skills were exceptional. I would come by the sales floor hearing laughter around the corner but there were customers near me waiting patiently. I should have known the laughter was her with other customers, making friends again.

That infectious laughter was soon transferred to planes and beaches working for the airline. That job was perfect. A new crew every week and a new batch of stories and friends. So many good people working in the skies, now more than ever when you're flying, show them they are valued, and depending on the airline, they're probably close friends of Mel. She often told me: "if you bring them a bag of sours or treats they can share, you'll get special treatment, just sayin."

Ask me my favorite moments with her and I can't single any out. I can only imagine all of it all over again. Sure, there are the obvious ones, holding our new babies in the hospital and laughter in our home all the time. But I feel blessed just to have known her and mad at myself for not treasuring her enough even though I know I did.

April 29

Chase had a drain put into his side to flow the fluids from around his heart. His heart rate was elevated and rising, and this will slow it enough to bring him out of danger. Still no results on the biopsy but it gives us time to pray for the best results. He has a possible diagnosis of Hodgkin's Lymphoma, and it is treatable with an extremely high success rate, but they can't conclusively say for 7-14 days. I love my boy so much and I know Mel would be devastated to know he's starting a battle like this. I also know she would be engaged in the situation researching, planning, and reassuring him and all of us that we'll get through this.

Doing a deep dive into Chases wall I picked out so many posts Mel sent to him, and they all touched the heart so well.

I see them in a whole different light now. Who wouldn't I guess, particularly her birthday wishes were always very eloquent and so personalized to the recipients. If you have some of them over the years, you'll know she has a way of making you feel empowered and so special. I was fortunate to be her earliest recipient well before the internet was installed in us all. She would pop by my work surprising me and would always leave me a letter sized love note folded into a well thought out shape almost like karagamii. I saved them all and there are plenty. Even at seventeen her writing was we'll worded and felt like a warm hug.

Everyone knows she has a special gift with words, spoken or written, and I was so proud of her when she graduated from U of R with a double major in History and English. She had many odds against her, challenging her struggle to graduate. We had the furniture store when she enrolled, and she stayed true to her studies while working the sales floor right through to the closure which was one of the hardest things for us to go through.

She continued while I was commuting to BC, her juggling motherhood and being a gate agent at the airport in Regina, she then commuted from BC after we moved and was suddenly broadsided in our suburban, it was quite a serious accident with her being angled out of the driver's window onto a stretcher, all showing just how tough she was and is.

I had my abilities, usually involving graphics and a computer, but I never had an interest in writing. I'm trying to pick up the torch and story tell the way I think she would want.

She's had trouble breathing all day yesterday and all night. She continues to have fluid buildup in her lungs. It's very hard to be here by her side, hearing the constant gurgle deep in her lungs. I can't imagine being anywhere else. I also have a peace that it won't be long. I've told her how much I love her and not to worry about me or the kids. I promised her I'd take good care of them.

I've thought a lot about my purpose lately. I believe I'm living it right now and have been for 30 years. It was my honor to care for her through this and I know we'll be together again one day in some form.

I'm reading a book called Imagine Heaven and it's helping me understand. We are on this earth to learn to love and teach others the importance to love also, truly love. Lately I've weeded out some hate and resentment, I realized there's no room in my orbit for any form of hate. A lot of people in the country, and the world, seem angry lately and I can only realize they've forgotten about unconditional love or never truly experienced it.

Chapter 8

April 30, 8:20am

Peace for Her

I'm sorry friends, Melanie has passed into a better life and is free of pain. She took her last breath a few minutes ago.

Time paused and the setting will live in my thoughts forever. The feeling I had can't be explained as I held her hand, my focus on her alone. I had noticed her breaths slowing, I had started a video of her friends from work speaking words of encouragement and stories of their fun times with her, the voices filled the room with a warmth which I'm sure comforted her.

The moment came and was gone as I witnessed her last breath and her transition into a better life. She is free of her pain now. Her passing paints a dark canvas on our side, a loss for us all but I'm comforted that on her side now, she is feeling pure love in her heavenly father's arms as the pain and fear have vanished, the ugly disease finally defeated. Our loss, in a way, can be seen as her win.

The moments after Mel passed, her mom came to sit with me at her bedside. It was brave of her and comforting for me in that moment. The room was peaceful now, quiet, void of the beeps and whirrs of machines, nurses no longer interrupting, checking vitals.

Almost 30 years ago Loralee and I had shared a Chinese meal as I asked for her daughter's hand. Now we shared this moment also, among tears and sobs we recounted all the way's Melanie was a blessing.

My parents gathered the strength and came also. At one point Mom asked how are you handling this difficult moment? My response was quick, surprising even myself, "Jesus is with me." She paused for a moment then smiled teary eyed saying "yes, I remember."

When I was six, little Randy wandered off in the department store like many kids do and when she found me, she asked that small boy "weren't you scared? ", it was my response then also.

Savannah, our daughter, also composed herself best she could to be with her mama one last time, and she needed that. Austin & Colby were very close to their mom but chose to not come. They needed to do what was right for them, wanting to preserve in their mind the living memory from their last visit. I respect their choice knowing we all have our own path in crisis moments.

Chase was in another hospital beginning his own battle and our prayers were also being sent up for him knowing Mel would know everything surrounding his challenge now, and surly much more.

The hours that followed are a blur, I remember packing up the room after family members came to be with me and have a last moment in her presence. I made two trips to the car emptying the room after they moved her to the morgue. Hours before they had dressed her in her favorite pink tie-dyed dress from Hawaii and did her hair so nicely. The care they showed was notable for our final moments as she laid at peace.

They instructed me to come back for the dress and wedding ring, picking those up at the nurses' station brought a sense of finality, the empathy of the nurses extending to me with hugs and well wishes. These caring souls, a special kind of person, heroes in fact, they were touched by Mel also in a unique way. They had witnessed our love story coming to its final chapter over the last few months. I had also observed their expertise in crisis moments when they had diverted her pain or avoided it altogether. These men and women deserve more credit than they are given.

In the last month Melanie wept frequently knowing that her world was going away. She felt like she had so much to do and say to the ones she loved. When she cried, I remember feeling guilty that I was often dry eyed while trying to comfort her. "I should have been more emotional too" I thought, but it makes sense now that she needed to see me being strong not falling apart so she could be confident everyone and everything would be taken care of.

Sav shared with me a few weeks earlier that she had secretly recorded Mel and I dancing at the many events we attended, and it was quite emotional to watch for me, but I noticed something I had never known because I was always looking in her eyes, but she would kick up her right heel quite gracefully while we danced. I'm so glad Sav did that and that's the lasting thought I'll have when I hear her favorite songs.

From this day on, I have a new connection to her. My only recourse, to believe she lives on in a spiritual form, If I don't embrace that, the link to her would truly be lost.

She is still around us. We will all have moments where we feel a connection to her, maybe seeing a rainbow or a beautiful sunset on a beach, rays of sunlight cast through the tree's, a bird, a butterfly, or even a moth. They're all valid forms of connection and all important to each of us in a very personal way.

I now have a new focus. For the last few days, I've been torn between two hospitals, Chase being treated in another city and country and my need to drive an hour away including a border crossing. I'll now shift my attention, giving him all my support.

I can't imagine his thoughts. He just lost his mother and couldn't pay her a last visit, living with grief and fear as he also laid in a hospital bed beginning his own new battle. When I see him, he looks well, up in spirits, but I know how he feels deep down, I feel it too.

Chapter 9

A Bit Brighter

May 1

Chase still had fluid around his heart caused by the mass in his lungs. He had a second surgery today to drain it from a lower area. Specialists are monitoring his heart rate closely and the pace was increasing. Explained to me: the sack around the heart is a fixed size, when fluid builds between it and the heart there's nowhere for the pressure to go, increasing his heartrate. If the pressure isn't relieved, it will be fatal. I also learned that this hospital had one of the top cardiac and vascular care wards in the state giving my boy an added advantage, thank God, we need success and hope right now more than ever.

I arrived minutes before the doctor ordered the emergency surgery allowing me to be a part of his escort down to the operating room. This was all happening so fast. I sat in the very quiet hallway, the lack of commotion landed thoughts of potential loss once again. How can this be my reality? How much can one man endure, how much can my boy and my surviving family endure?

"Mister Regier" a voice drew my face out of my palms as I looked up to see a man in a suit. "I'm the head administrator of the hospital, nice to meet you" I obliged, standing and shaking his outstretched hand. "It's been brought to my attention you lost your wife yesterday and your son is now in surgery. I want to offer my dearest condolences and let you know we're doing all we can to make this day a bit brighter for you. The doctor is just finishing up and the surgery went very well."

I was overcome with emotion as I tried to carry a conversation. Recognizing my need for privacy, he turned and walked away after asking if I needed a soda or anything at all. The top admin in the hospital asking if he could get me something, I was touched. A year ago, I would have sought out a stiff drink to numb my reality, today I was given grace by a divine power I presume. "Prayer from my family & friends was helping me through" I thought to myself.

I was up like a shot when the porter pushed Chase's stretcher through the automatic doors. My boy, bearing a weak smirk as our eyes signaled to each other that all was well. The walk up to his room did seem a bit brighter, as promised.

His surgery went very well, and the doctor is pleased. He'll have the new drain in for 48hrs if the fluid drains and removed when they're confident of it's success.

I'm certain Mel is watching over and asking God to guide doctors and nurses to properly care for her baby.

I'm grateful to you all for your caring words in the comments, I feel your pain also. Be kind to yourself today. Love the ones around you a little extra.

May 3

Chase's drain has been successful, and we can focus on getting him home to rest up. The doctors will remove it tomorrow sometime. Thanks for all your support and the prayers for him. They're so important right now. He's feeling much better, and his girlfriend Aimee is stepping in where I just can't right now.

Hearing all the reports from the doctors is hard for me to deal with so soon. Emotionally I've been strained over the last three years, a roller coaster of events surrounding Melanie's treatments and surgeries. Aimee has proven worthy of this role for Chase when I needed her. Comprehending and relaying information when I can't be there, raising questions with the doctors that I may have missed when I am in the meetings also.

I'm sharing a love txt Mel sent me on February 14th when she was in VGH for valentine's day. I brought her flowers and sour candy. I don't have many recent love txt's because we did them in person which I preferred; Now I wish more were documented.

I'm also sharing some photos which I've adapted to the nail polish rack I got her for Christmas. I sleep on her side of the bed so I can feel closer to her and the pictures, and the tissues. She was such an excellent mother, always putting the kids first, planning outings above yard or housework. Vacations were always as a family, the first one as a couple was when the kids were already teens.

Twelve Loving Weeks turned out to be three, I feel like we were shorted time promised. She kept saying to the doctors "it ain't over till the fat lady sings, right?" They always looked a bit confused and just said a dry "Yah" not sure how to respond, but we knew Mel's humor and the moment was perfection.

If she could say something to you all I imagine it would be funny for sure, a mix of sarcasm and some shock-valued remark that only she could deliver. It would end with a bit of sweetness, assurance and finally lots of hearts bursting with love for each of you. She would want you to embrace everyone around you, yes, your family and kids and dogs & cats & bunnies but reach out to strangers who she always saw as undiscovered friends. That's why there's so damn many of you!

She was such a free spirit living among us, an angel all along and we didn't see it fully. I'll try to reply to some of your texts wanting to help your hurting hearts and give you a chuckle the way she would. There's so much love pouring in, and I can't possibly respond to you all, but know that I appreciate so much your kindness. I see that it comes directly from the warmest part of your hearts.

My legal name is Randell, I've been Randy all my life, but she never called me that except a couple of times right before she passed. It was always Rand. Her whole family calls me that and close friends too. I never thought much of it. Now I want to go by Rand and say, "people close to me call me that", and when they do I think of her in a subtle way.

At the end of the love txt, she wrote "don't fall," it was in reference to one time back when we were dating, I was saying "I love you" while walking out of the living room and my shoe caught the phone cord sending me into a graceful but noticeable recovery of all but my dignity. She... yup burst out laughing but said I love you too among her chuckles. Over the years I'd fake a trip saying it just to bring us back to that fun moment.

Dear hero

I want to tell you how incredible you are! I love you more than life!

You are my best friend! You have saved me repeatedly and I have no words for how I feel about you!

I will always love you beyond anything.

You are my heart, my soul, my laughter and my spirit!

Thank you for being you!!!

Xoxoxo

Ps. Don't fall

-Mel

I Loved you the instant we met.

You always warm my heart with a simple hello and your beautiful smile.

I'm privileged to be closest to your sunshine

I Love You

-Rand

May 4

I have a good update on Chase. He's home from the hospital walking around steady on his feet and glad to be back with his siblings and his furry friend Cooper. He'll be receiving chemo soon, but they've assured us it'll be a short term and not to worry. Still no word on a conclusive diagnosis but we're trusting they're being thorough. Thanks for all the warm regards and prayers.

Chapter 10

Go Away Bags

May 5

"Captain butter cup and first officer sweat pea" was a common introduction made by the sweet voice of Melanie Regier right before landing on many flights. Unknown to the pilots the guests would file out past them smiling and chuckling, some of them asking "are you buttercup or sweat pea?"

I missed her when she was away as I do now. When loading up her "go away bags" I called them, she would tell me not to sulk. I knew she didn't really want to leave me or the peaceful home we made but we did have to pay the bills and I did have to share her sunshine. I would take comfort that the hour drive was our special time and often we would make a sushi stop to make up for a missed date night.

Our wedding was simple but special too. The outdoor ceremony planned among the breathtaking flowers and cobblestone paths at Minter Gardens were subject to rainfall, even though our research proved it hadn't rained on that day for 10 years. We resorted to a covered area with her, me and the pastor directly below the gift shop sign shown plainly in our wedding album.

I never realized but it was quite suiting to have "gift" displayed boldly above my bride. I know she'd want me to stop talking about her so much right now. She was never one to flaunt. Going through our many home videos she would often look to me when I panned away from the kids then to her, she'd go from a smile to an annoyed stance saying "stop." I knew what that meant and usually obliged. I wish I could go back and explain "I'll need these one day."

May 6

By now you're probably thinking this dude's heart is shattered. It is but I'm also feeling ok. I may be sharing stories that most people would consider to be private, but I'm realizing I need this to be out there and having an outlet like this is definitely helping me cope. As I "live stream" my emotion, I hope it's encouraging you to look around and see the beauty in your surroundings and embrace the people you love.

Our apartment is newer with white cabinetry and marble countertops, light colored walls and trim. It's a little fancy for me but I wanted to do that for Mel for our last few months she had, and we both hoped the gym and the pool would aid in our sliver of hope that she may recover provided a miracle.

We never were very good with yard work and neglected a budget for landscaping when we had enjoyment of each other and the kids to invest in. Now I'm thankful for the choices we made, to enjoy life when we could. The memories are the dividends I now hold dearly.

Now, my head rests on my pillowy bed as my eyes gather the nightly scene from our bank of large windows. I started leaving the blinds open at night so I can see the courtyard path with its mood lights casting soft lumens onto the green grass and perfectly clipped shrubbery.

The emerald streetlight changes to amber and ruby all night long as I lay in bed with my live photograph while I drift away. Having the visual connection to the stars and the universe is comforting right now.

I gave notice for the end of the month so I can get something a little more practical and be closer to the kids, but I'm glad I can have this moment, peaceful and serene.

Chapter 11

Cow Purse

May 9

The last 365 days were gifts given to us since Mel was told she had only two years to live with treatment and we received three. I'm grateful but one always wants a little more. It would have been nice if she had just lived past Mother's Day or her upcoming birthday. Mother's Day came quickly as I've been caught up with the selection of photos and home videos searching for those few perfect moments, I'll share with her many friends at 1:00 pm on May 27th, her memorial, also her birthday.

I originally set out to look at scanners and a better computer so I can present the highest resolution and achieve the best polished tribute. Weaving through parking lots and aisles of too much selection I made a common realization among dads. With Mother's Day coming tomorrow, a gathering planned by her sister Katherine, it became an urgency and a separate honoring of mothers dear to me.

Mel wasn't big on gifts for herself but always wanted meaningful ones for others to show the depth of her caring nature. I had a new mission now and different parking lots to conquer for the mothers needing my focus.

There was one time a gift was important to Mel; we had been dating since St. Patrick's Day and we were a couple for 77 days and her birthday was her first with me. Back then I wandered the aisles of Woolco and Eaton's landing what I thought was the perfect gift.

Nope, disappointed was all over her face as she tried to mask her feelings. My prized offering of a black and white purse with an outer surface of applied short hair in a pattern, much like a dairy cow, was not what she was expecting or could appreciate. It was suddenly the most awful site in the room. Her family members knew I had failed but tried to show support as they casually exited the room no doubt to chuckle around the corner. Mel also excused herself to her room with a quivering voice saying something like "it's ok, you meant well"

We never talked about what she was hoping for that day but I'm sure now it was probably a ring and me on a knee. The cow-purse was a comical reference for many years, proving it had value after all.

The proposal did happen weeks later at the base of bridal falls near Chilliwack on a viewing deck which is now erased from the mountain side. I had planned much better for this presentation and had her ring hidden in a cooler mixed with sandwiches and cookies. The moment was perfection in my mind as I kissed her then dropped down searching for my lost prize in the cooler. What are you doing? She asked. Just a moment... as I finally handled it with relief. Then the unexpected, a man tapped my shoulder and a voice in broken English says, "you take pictures for me?" "Oh, sure" I replied. Upon completion of their photo shoot, I continued, and they were witness to me dropping on one knee for my plea. Cheers and applause erupted as Mel said "yes, now get up!" Those foreigners were etched into the script that day providing yet another comical part to our story.

Yesterday was our kids first Mother's Day without their mom, it wasn't easy for any of us, but she would want us to take comfort that she's gathered with many great mothers in glory who our families all adored. Shelly, Doreen, Diane, Elaine, Agnes and Mary all celebrating with much laughter, I'm sure.

Savannah, Austin, Colby and Chase, your mother loved you so much. She wanted and fought hard to be here for you. We'll all be together with her one day and it will be amazing.

Chapter 12

Cherished Breaths

May 13

I've gone back many times in my mind to the day we found out that we were going to have our first baby which turned out was our only sweet girl, Savannah. Mel asked me to take her to the clinic because she had stomach flu like symptoms, and she just didn't feel right. I agreed instantly even though I had just worked an all-nighter and needed sleep badly.

I waited in the car at her request and when she came out, she sat slowly in her seat looking shell-shocked. Rand? I'm pregnant. She seemed a bit scared and hesitant to look at me directly, but her mood was instantly changed when I erupted with joy.

I'm going to be a dad? I mean we're going to be parents, together? I remember saying "I love kids. I'm actually pretty good with them." Thinking back that was a corny thing to say. At that moment I knew we were going to be the couple that would bond together and create a loving home. Those were such good years. Whenever I see young families it's hard not to be a bit jealous and the Trace Atkins song "you're goanna miss this" comes to mind.

One theme I'm seeing as I look through all our photos is Mel with her chin on their shoulder from behind, not posing but really engaged like she was taking in their presence with cherished breaths. Being a mommy to those little ones was one of her true callings and she did it well. She was always the flight attendant who would relieve the weary moms on the flights bouncing their bundles up the aisles and spoiling kids with treats teaching them to say please and thank-you in the process.

It's disappointing for me to know I'll never witness her being a grandma. We always said how we were going to be that cute old couple in our 80's holding hands at Mill Lake giving visual encouragement to middle-aged couples, affirmation that love can last if you let it.

I thank God I had the time I did with her. She taught me to truly love. I know I did with her but I'm not sure I can do what she did with others, complete strangers? I'm not usually the one to strike up awkward conversation turning it into a lasting friendship, that was her thing, and I was always along for the ride, that fun ride.

Chapter 13

A Lot of Information

May 16

It's quiet now, I hate it, but I love it. I feel more connected to God, my emotions, and her memory. That's all I have now, times of reflection, and that part is also hard. Oh, she was a chatterbox at times, she knew it, and we joked about it too. One time I was practicing "selective hearing" I called it, she caught me, there was no recovery, I had been saying "uh-huh, yep, hmm" all at the right que's while watching one of my car-guy shows, but I missed content she was now quizzing me on.

"You're not even listening to me, and this is important stuff I'm telling you." My only response was honesty. "You do give me a lot of information."

That one line resurfaced for years, she wasn't mad like she could have been, she knew she talked a lot and we both knew she couldn't do anything about it, nor would I want her to. Now I certainly miss her "information" and I regret tuning out all those other times. What I wouldn't give... I should have at least thrown my recorder on, stupid. I search for her voice in our home videos and that's all I have. I tried saving her voicemails but didn't do it well enough.

Boston Pizza 30 years and a few months ago I was facing a plate of appies and my roommate's ex-girlfriend, comforting her after their break-up.

A sip of my long island iced tea was accompanied by the first time I had the realization "Melanie sure talks a lot." Not in a bad way, I saw how engaging she was, how she radiated excitement and a unique style of storytelling, evident even then at seventeen.

I was seeing her in a new light although the thought of dating her hadn't crossed my mind, she was merely a friend who needed a listening ear, and I was trying to be a good person while trying not to get involved in the politics of their stressful situation. She was touching on points a girl would naturally have touted but it was missing some elements, sadness, and despair.

She was still the bubbly girl Wayne and I had gone to dinner with just a week ago. I had sat down prepared to face tears, anger, and questions I couldn't answer. Instead, we were having pleasant conversation, laughter even. She was only confused about one thing, "he had broken up with her", she hadn't had this rejection before. That seemed to be her biggest complaint. "Well of course" I realize now, Melanie always got the first job she applied for, decided when she was moving on and now has a bountiful collection of friends. Her perplexity over one rejection must have completely baffled her.

Weeks before, Mel & Wayne, my good friends/roommate/couple, had been trying to find me a girlfriend so we could do double dates instead of this weird three musketeer act. Her quest for finding me someone even involved the owner of the Italian restaurant and their daughter, which thankfully never happened.

That trio had gone out quite a few times and I guess they just felt sorry for me at first, didn't want me left out of their date night. It became more of a regular thing when we all realized we had too much fun together. I suppose Wayne also realized he had transitioned to a third wheel at some point.

Lucky me, I had been summoned to damage control, comforting a friend in her transition but there seemed to be something else there. The days went on with me picking her up from Woolco where she worked the counter of the smoke shop which also housed a variety of racks of magazines which she (we) had to inventory every night. Stacks of magazines along with cigar and cigarette brands were carefully counted while loading them into shopping carts then taken to the back room where the valuables would be secure. I was doing a loathed part of her job; I wasn't getting a paycheck, but it did give me more time with her even though I was the target of a scheme much like huck fin would conspire. Now, I realize it was also a test and I suppose I passed.

My counseling sessions turned into walks at Mill Lake late at night then romance and a strong bond which I wasn't expecting but had to have.

Our first official date was St. Patrick's Day. I had planned a dinner at a local Irish pub that had advertised a special act and an Irish theme. I remember Melanie's black sequin dress, as I opened the restaurant door, I placed my hand on her lower back while she entered. When I did, she turned her head glancing at me almost to speak, her eyes knowing something. Then she turned and walked as we were brought to our table.

The pub was alive with voices and laughter, a pianist revved the atmosphere as the Celtic singer applied her talent using a bright green boa going table to table lacing it over the shoulders of red-faced men as they offered shrugs to their dates.

"She'd better not come here" Mel said sternly, only too late as the singer tapped my shoulder with her feathery wand. Mel smiled firm-lipped at her, eyebrows raised like only she could do, intending to shew away the annoyance which promptly worked as the woman targeted another table. "Jealous much"? I said, queuing her turn to wear a blushed smile. "Yes, in fact" was her response with a full-on smile, surprising me and her in the moment but there it was, "her jealous," it meant something.

It was days later, she admitted to me the "glance" she gave me in the entrance was the result of tingles she felt when my hand guided her into the restaurant. It must have been significant for her to reference it every year following. Now I realize it must have been the "luck of the charm" for me that night.

We dated officially for a few weeks and suddenly she broke up with me. She never said exactly why but it was the hardest two-week adjustment I ever experienced. We were meant to be together, why didn't she see that?

Persistence paid off when I finally got my chance to present my closing remarks on her stairway and from that point, I gladly subjected myself to decades of hearing her lively conversation.

I lied, this is the hardest two-week adjustment I've ever had to make, I don't know what I'd do if she hadn't blessed me with four beautiful children. I promised her I would take care of them, and I said I would be ok. Now it's up to me to muster up my own sunshine I can spread to others like she would do.

Chase is doing quite well, puppy therapy helps (Daisy) I realized our home needed some joy right now and so did Cooper. Chase's diagnosis was in fact Hodgkin's lymphoma, and he'll start chemo soon maybe in a week or two as soon as they wean back the steroids being used to suppress the mass in his lung. He'll have 6 months of treatment through a port in his chest twice a month for a 3 or 4 hr. infusion. He has his appetite back and is feeling stronger. They have great success treating this disease and many sources say they know lots of people who have a normal long life afterwards.

Thank you for your prayers and your well wishes of encouragement. Rather than responding to each of you I'm going to put my time into writing this story. I hope you don't mind. I feel it's the best tribute to Mel, maybe I can help some of you dealing with hardship or open your eyes to the beauty and love you're surrounded with.

May 20

I Dreamt I was at home waiting for her to come back. She wasn't working but had come and left to see some friends, but she was gone too long. I was getting frustrated, so I was looking for my keys and phone to go out also, and just drive anywhere.

Bounding from room to room, keys are gone and my phone? I decided to look upstairs in our room which I had to go outside to access, started scaling the wall but it was too high. Oh, right I'll just use the stairs I had built. Yaa this is too weird to not be a dream... Ok lights? On & quick off when I saw her bundled under the covers breathing heavy like she was in the hospital. She was home all along what a relief. Feeling stupid for getting angry at her then almost waking her, then *me* waking up to realize she really is gone.

I feel like I've changed as a person, I can't be the same, act the same or experience life the same way I did when she was around. It's bound to be different, that's inevitable. But I was meant to be the other part of a couple, a team in so many ways now I'm one half of what I was. A big part of me is missing.

Looking at our wedding video made me wish I could just hold both her hands again and see her face as she smiles at me with those beautiful lips and her loving eyes. I watch that moment engaged, memorizing her every move. I was blessed to have that moment and maybe it made me have a dream the following night that she came to me holding both my hands, we were facing each other once more but this was different. Both our hands were glowing yellow with warmth flowing up down and around, then over again, our hands were moving through each other. I dreamt more about her, but I can't remember. I hope to have her in my dreams tonight and that I remember.

We had plans to take up living room dancing and I had a country style program I had signed up for so we could do it right but still in the privacy of our hideaway apartment.

The dancing was set to start when she was discharged and we did have 2 weeks plus a few days in our place to kick up our heels with newly purchased boots she picked out for inspiration, hers pink with too many rhinestones but still not enough. The plan ultimately was to surprise our guests at our 30th anniversary celebration July 5th this year. So close.

The drug regiment spoiling our dance nights. That must be accepted now. And her plan of lifting the wedding dress to reveal her sparkling boots won't happen on this earth. But we can all imagine how proud she would have been, and I can hope to see some version of those boots one of these sleep-filled nights.

Chapter 14

I Broke your Car

May 21

A beautiful capture of the view from my bed this morning, bright sunlight striking the greenery outside and the white duvet on my bed, cloud-like matching the sky. This along with a glorious 5-hour sleep was a welcomed event since my nights have been broken lately.

Yesterday was a good day. "We should have donuts" my sweet little niece Momo once said with her elbows perched comfortably on her inflated purple pool on a day much like this. We've used that phrase often since and it's always made the family laugh but for me it's like a lesson spoken from the mouth of babes to always appreciate the good moments, they can suddenly be there happening around us in such a subtle moment then gone.

My birthday was different without Mel, but I did my best to make it a good day. After an always enjoyable brunch with my parents, I went to the track in Mission to watch some muscle thundering the 1/4-mile track where I met a new friend, the only other soul in the stands who turned out to be a remarkable human. I don't usually strike up conversations, that's what Mel would do, and I realize the reward has value.

To get there I chose to drive through the Matsqui flats which reminded me of a day when we were still dating. Mel had borrowed my prized 88 Camaro to take her friends for a joy ride in the flats where there were no other cars, and the roads are paved. She thought she had pushed the car too hard showing off to her friends when a buzzer like sound came from below. Cutting the ride short and dropping her friends off she returned sheepishly saying I'm sorry, I broke your car. Puzzled by her description I sourced the odd noise to the console where I had my battery powered shaver ready for quick touch ups, it and had randomly turned on. Another story providing a chuckle whenever a car was acting odd, did you check the console?

Thank you everyone for your supportive heartfelt birthday wishes, I really do appreciate you all right now

Spending these last few weeks working solely on the tribute slideshow, the program and Journaling has widened my understanding of who I was actually married to if that's even possible by now. "I thought I loved you then" as Brad Paisley puts it.

Friends of hers have contacted me who I've never met, or I haven't seen for a while telling me how Mel helped them through a very dark valley they were going through. This is happening frequently and I'm realizing I may never know how many lives she has impacted and still is.

The memorial is in two days and I'm feeling drained emotionally. I've been able to focus on her tribute turning various areas of the apartment into production centers. Learning video editing software has been challenging but an essential part of what I feel in my heart I must do. She said once that she didn't want a funeral but rather a celebration where everyone would be laughing not walking around sad, crying at triggers unexpectedly as I've been rehearsing for. Honoring her for me has been examining her presence and involvement in her orbit especially the last three years.

She was so family based and I always appreciated the way she was close with all of them, and they always welcomed me into the fold. Honoring them on her tribute day is especially important to me now.

Honor extends to her WestJet family and close friendships that were forged, they are also my family, and I must embrace every one of them who she cared so dearly for.

A little over a month ago I took her wedding dress in to have it dry cleaned and they wouldn't do it due to the age being 30 years. Of course, it was only worn once in my mind it was practically new. The memory of our honeymoon is still fresh like last week. We road tripped our way through Roger's pass stopping at Three Valley Gap -Lake Chateau Inn where they had a cave room.

The special room was lined with rock, featuring a waterfall shower flowing into a crafted pond-like tub. It was romantic and special. We continued through Alberta where she skillfully slalomed around a car sized straw bale right in the middle of the freeway as I woke up in the passenger seat.

Her wedding dress was now pressed, not cleaned but ready for pickup along with black pants I gathered thinking they were mine and the boys could wear them to our 30th. The pants ended up being hers, part of her work costume as her mom calls it. Mel thought it was cute how her profession was seen by her mom as a play. I couldn't make our young men wear girl pants to her funeral now so with pride I outfitted them with a successful trip to the local Men's shop.

When I picked up her dress back then it hung angelically, high in the rafters between the mini sky-rail of plastic shrouded clothing traveling endlessly around the ceiling. The train of her dress looked longer than I expected and when the owner fished it down with a long pole, I was overcome. I watched as his team of professionals folded it with care and placed it in the keepsake dress box with precision and grace.

At the time Mel was waiting in the truck as I emerged from the entrance smiling as I presented her the showcased trophy made of linen and beads. She was so proud.

Chapter 15

Rocket Girl

May 29

"Rocket Girl" I've been pranked. Maybe my own doing or maybe she wanted to see me laugh. I choose door number two. I felt compelled on her birthday, two days ago the day of her memorial, to wish my Melanie a happy birthday sending it up to her enjoying that new celestial home. I do my stories in my note's app on my phone and usually type a topic throughout the day to embellish later. I wrote her the birthday wish, selected all, copied and pasted it on her wall proofreading way too late.

There it was, Rocket girl, leading the paragraph like I was mocking her one last time and it was perfection but not my intention and probably made a few head scratches out there. We had enjoyment regarding the song by Doc Walker where he talks about her "flying him out of this world." She lists all the places she had flown to, but he knew that she hadn't. Mel, before becoming a flight attendant, was that girl when she would announce a trip I knew we couldn't afford earning the nickname which I opportunely nudged her about from time to time.

Then the day came when she was flying away weekly, and I took pleasure to join her when it worked out, usually a lot of flying with only one beach day but I didn't mind I was with my soul's partner and got spoiled while she worked the aisle of the 737. My eyes were opened to the part of her job she loved, the flight crew. Many fun nights with laughter over dinner & drinks, long walks and visits on the beach late into the night with everyone hearing but not seeing the waves creeping closer, the warm wind carrying our laughter to the stars. I now enjoyed the benefits of my rocket girl.

Our first Maui trip was a head scratcher itself. She was a new employee for the airline, a gate agent, and we couldn't believe we now could fly to a beach on a company's dime. Arriving at the airport I was amazed how they didn't need corridors that protected us from extreme cold like I was used to in central Canada. I still had my snow coat on and looked like an idiot.

We got our bags and went for the cab saying take us to our condo in Kauai, we were in Kahului. You know that's another island, replied the driver. Hmm the ad we picked the condo from said Maui, Kauai and I assumed State/City...I didn't need my snow coat to embarrass me at that moment.

Is there a ferry maybe? Nope you need a plane. With a few failed calls to Condo Bob, he was no help and couldn't, wouldn't refund us having no pity for the new "homeless people in paradise" his words. Night was coming before any available flights so time to thumb through brochures and beg for mercy.

We had very little cash back then. We had just sold our house and were waiting for escrow to drop money into our account. Her mom did us a solid and floated us a life ring, thanks again mom!

Our new condo was in a remote town, and we hiked for our groceries and some liquid treats for which I picked lemons from the tree out back. We made it special like we always did, sometimes the best trips are the ones you have the most challenges on. We talked about that trip many times over the years. And we got our islands memorized also.

Update on Chase

We sat through a detailed meeting with Chase's cancer doctor today road mapping his 6-month treatment which is starting next Wednesday. He'll be having a pic-line inserted tomorrow and should be able to attend his mom's tribute. He's booked up heavily with tests and appointments until then. They wanted to start his infusions the day of her memorial, but when they heard, they agreed it could wait three more days, although the doctor could see an advancing threat.

It's all happening fast but I'm very impressed with his care so far. Thanks for continuing to pray for him, we really do appreciate you all.

June 1

Its week eight of our twelve loving weeks. I can feel the love that's been coming our way from all of you, and I really appreciate it. Chase is starting his chemo at this moment. He's in good spirits and all is going well. They've allowed two of us in the infusion bay. Aimee, his girlfriend, and me but I know Mel is here also. Please say a prayer for him as we enter this new journey.

June 3

"You're not funny" Mel often said to me when newlyweds, usually with an under toned giggle, as I would test the waters with a quick-witted comment. Perfecting my Rand humor since I was five for this sole purpose, I knew If I got a chirp when she laughed, I was owning the room.

Making someone belly laugh for any of us is a rewarding experience and in Mel's circles it was often accomplished rebounding between friends or family like it was her own little sitcom.

Her laughter response is now one of the things I'm missing most. That and holding her until my arm falls asleep.

I still laugh at times, still continue the wise cracks with my boys, they come as a reflex at this point. I just miss making *her* laugh. I miss how good it made me feel giving her that pleasure especially when she was going through so much in the last few years.

One of her friends (Caroline) brought her a keychain from Hawaii with a metal M about two months before her passing and it had a nice soft jingle to it with the tiny bell along with the island themed charms. She hadn't driven for about 6 months, and it wasn't used for the intended keys. I frequently picked it up playing with it hearing its fairy like tune in the quiet moments while Mel slept and eventually started hanging it from my pocket hearing its subtle jingle as we walked the halls together or when I went on errands.

I still hang it from my pocket, and it reminds me she's still at my side and is helping in some way as I find my new path in life, it's a simple but meaningful connection to her.

I want to say something about her care she received at the various hospitals, St. Paul's, VGH, Royal Columbian but most importantly Abbotsford Regional and the Cancer clinic. The palliative care unit at ARH really left a positive impression with Mel and I, as well as our whole family. The genuine care each Doctor, Nurse or Care aid displayed was touching.

These people have given their hearts, sacrificed their bodies, denied their own sleep or time with family to provide this loving effort to make our experience the best it can be knowing the likely outcome would be grim. I know like a lot of hospitals now. They're operating short staffed and running on fumes.

We've called them heroes, banged pots out our windows and applied stickers to our cars but not many get a full visual of the challenges they subject themselves to every day. All this and they must have to insulate themselves from bearing grief after witnessing human tragedy on a daily basis. Annie, Schayne, Neelam, Elaine, Kat and so many more who personally gave extra, beyond what was required of themselves. Thank you.

If you know someone in this type of vocation let them know how valued they are and how I personally want to thank them from the perspective of a loved one.

Chapter 16

Home Security

June 7

Today I had a morning dream, I was at a political gathering just waiting for some young teens I had brought to come down to the lobby. My mind wandering, eyes aimlessly scanning the room and up to the balcony there she was, Mel with her hair tied back, it was brown though, not the usual blonde but her natural color. She was wearing a formal dark dress just standing alone staring at nothing then at me, was that Mel? She's beautiful I thought to myself, then I said it. "You're so beautiful, you've always been beautiful." She half smiled not saying anything in reply while gracefully walking away. I woke up feeling alone but satisfied, I had seen her.

Reality. 1998 Regina, we had just moved there, and I had to travel back to Abbotsford to get the rest of our boxes and leftover things that wouldn't fit in the small cube van. Road tripping with my dad in his RV, our plan was a quick turnaround renting a trailer there and head back. A few challenges before returning involving everything closed on a Sunday and the rear bumper welded back on. You can guess.

Finally, home reunited with Mel and the kids in the back yard I noticed something peculiar. Finishing nails applied halfway into the top of the fence in a quite un-professional way, where someone nefarious might try to climb over. Hun, what's this? Embarrassed she explained her obvious reason and pointed out the cooking oil poured down the planked rows and aluminum cans she had lined up on the ground provided the intruder was successful.

The movie "Home Alone" came to mind, no doubt in yours too, I'm glad she didn't have a forgotten can of paint swing-anchored to the roof gable. My poor wife felt vulnerable caring for our three small kids, at the time, in a new neighborhood and she acted on her concerns. Never mentioned it to me but didn't try to conceal anything either. Well noted. I made sure she felt safe going forward.

We wasted a full year getting to know our forever friends Brent and Sherry across the alleyway who also would have given her assurance if we had known them yet.

I was excited to work with my dad -Sam at his furniture store with two locations. I was learning the ropes and how to be a manager as well as lending my adapted knowledge of marketing and advertising. Mel would often surprise me with a visit and show the kids what daddy did when I was away for the day.

The stores grew and expanded but after 7 years we endured the hardship of closing them and I became a truck driver for about a year with the thought of going up to Fort Mac to make larger dollars the next year. I spent my day delivering farm chemicals and seed to small towns all over southern Saskatchewan usually gone for the maximum 14 hours as a day driver.

We weren't allowed to have passengers, but I missed her while I drove endlessly. I decided to bend the rules a few times and stow her away in the bunk until I was caught by a fellow driver passing me near Davidson. That morning I had picked her up at a predetermined gravel road outside Regina hiding her in the sleeper until I was sure we wouldn't get caught. We were headed out when a young girl climbed out of the ditch. Thinking she was in distress I opened the passenger door to hear her out. "I have to get a ride to Yorkton, and I'll do anything to get there." That's all Mel needed to hear, flinging back the curtains emerging from the bunk she shocked the young thing saying, "this driver has a lover already," and truly I did.

"Melanie" -a name that signifies a freedom-loving and free-spirited individual. Nothing is conventional with your love of change and adventure. You make sensible decisions very quickly, especially in a dangerous or difficult situation.

June 10

Today it happened, my first flight after Melanie left this earth. I'm on my way to see the Roughriders first home game of the season and it's going to be fun enjoying it with the sea of green and my great friends Jeff and Barry. Also meeting up with Brent & Sherry, Rhonda & Wayne.

As we take off it feels slightly different. I flew many times with Mel either at my side or a call button away, but there's a new appreciation of how the mountains majestically present the variety of beauty and expanse, the cumulus clouds blanket past the horizon rowed up like cotton balls. It's not hard to imagine at this moment her spirit, ascending towards the bright sky and beyond the atmosphere 42 days ago.

She loved and hated her job flying. The love part involved lasting connections with good, good people I've found even now lending support and so many hugs in person or virtually on the day of her memorial. I was honored that so many took the time to come out seeking a lasting part of her. The attendance was well over 150 and another 100 or so virtually, I know she would agree, that's a lot of love in one room.

Pilots had asked if they could wear uniforms, being sensitive, not wanting to be a distraction. "It would make me and her proud" I said, choking me up each time. Just the thought of having them there with their stripes and badges appearing randomly among the crowd added a regard to how special she was.

In the earlier days when I would travel with her while she worked, I would be kind of awe struck around the pilots. She thought it was funny, like they were rock stars or something, but I couldn't help it. I just had a respect for how they had achieved their life passion and now they were taking on the responsibility of hundreds of lives each day, not really thinking much about it.

Eventually I was able to overcome and got to know many of them as I joined her for trips. The crews would mingle for drinks and dinner in paradise, or some less fortunate destination. I saw a side of the pilots that brought a certain level of comfort. There's a code among many of them during the layovers where they tend to umbrella the flight attendants, keeping them from harm. Really caring beyond the confines of the occupation. It really helped me know that even though she was thousands of miles away she was being guarded.

She did her traveling & exploring for work the last eight years and when she was home, she was rooted in and I couldn't usually get her to go out for so much as a dinner. Picking her up from the Vancouver airport was a regular event and always good to be reunited but also sleep was most likely warranted on the drive home. I know she had enjoyed herself maybe a little too much sometimes, but I was satisfied to have her once again on my arm perched over the console giving me the feeling of a barbarian king. I knew these days were limited since she was seeing the next stage of her career. We both knew this wasn't sustainable, being apart so much, missing each other all the time. This had to come to some sort of an end.

Her/our favorite road trip was down the Oregon coast stopping often to see either the sea lion caves or just wander the ocean shores. On our last trip we rented quads and hit the dunes, highly recommended. She was even feeling well enough to take one for a rip. I plan to take our family crew this summer and really enjoy hoping she'll somehow see us, hoping we'll feel some part of her there with us too.

June 20

We enjoyed watching our kids in sports, lacrosse was their game exclusively. I'm a football/hockey fan but lacrosse has a different skill set which is to be admired. Many trips out to various far away towns brought Mel and I much enjoyment not only the fact of a road trip but watching our Chase, an excellent goalie, brave the hard balls being hurled like small missiles seeking the goal he guarded with a quick eye and a fast reflex, his shield and tool, a different type of goalie stick with many knots strategically placed in the oversized head.

Mel was also a skilled lacrosse mom at the sidelines, cheering, encouraging and foul calling. As the game climaxed so would her pacing and when a "W" was accomplished Chase was always rewarded with a pile-up of jerseys and gear-clad hugs from his celebrating team mates often ending up on the ground with all of them.

Halftime, gave us moments to collect our composure and address our plans for the trip back, check our phones, see what reality would remind us of. I was doing just that when a text popped up asking who I was and why I called him? Sorry stranger, I didn't call you after checking my outgoing. Wasn't even a pocket dial. "I can prove it" said he presenting a screen shot of his incoming. Back and forth it went and I couldn't see the sense of continuing and he wouldn't let it go. Showing Mel, she presented a quick solution taking my phone and replying, "you sure call your mom a lot." It was true I hadn't picked that up, but she sure did and then I had major damage control on my hands. Typical of Mel to find humor and get someone in trouble in the process.

Chase always did us proud working his craft in the games and my favorite play he brilliantly executed was a backwards shovel pass blindly over his head with opposing players charging from all directions.

Unknowingly he assisted a goal that play earning his chocolate shake, extra whip cream on the way home.

Chase has had two chemo treatments now and is doing well. He'll have a total of 6 months twice per month. His swelling has greatly reduced in his lymph nodes in his neck. He's opted to a smooth top shave after hair loss began on que but he's fine with it being the only side effect. Thanks for all your love and support.

Chapter 17

It's a Baby

June 27

Mel's last writing spoke volumes about her heart for others. We had just been moved from Vancouver General to Abbotsford Regional Hospital and she had made quick friends with the nurses as usual, asking about their lives and drawing mental images of ours using her unique story telling conversation. I often listened to her chatting while being ported away for another MRI or radiation treatment and she would immediately ask the porter "so how's your day going"? Small talk is common but with Mel I always noticed a genuine interest in others even when she was going through a living hell, and I know she was terrified in the back of her mind. I often stood by helpless while she talked, encouraging herself, "ok, you can do this", "this is easy", but I knew how much pain she was having.

I helped when I could, bringing anything she wanted to her bedside, setting up and taking down her walker repeatedly. Going to a series of restaurants, stores, and drive through's trying to bring her anything that would give her comfort. We were both so grateful when the nurses arranged a second bed in the room so I could wheel it up right beside her like we were back home in our bedroom. Our favorite time was the evening as she would drift off, head on my shoulder.

When I was at the racetrack shortly after she passed, I made a new friend like she would often do, and we shared common stories of cancer heartaches. He said something that almost shocked me. A lot of partners walk away from a dying spouse or partner. This amazed me. How could someone simply disconnect. And how could they go on in life knowing they walked away when the one they love suffered. I'm so glad God gave me the strength to be there for her.

Our first hospital experience 29 years prior was the debut of our beautiful Savannah Lee. Mel was in labor, and I had gone out to get her some McDonald's breakfast wraps at her request. I returned just as the show was about to begin. I think I can speak for most men that our mind does strange things when facing this stressful situation and my only thought at the moment was, I couldn't let the wraps get cold and she was saying how hungry she was just 30 minutes ago. The doctor and nurses were preparing the room so I efficiently prepared one with hot sauce the way she liked them and even though she said to give her one I realized she wouldn't be eating anything as Doctor Burns looked at me like I had clearly lost my marbles. "This is happening now Rand." Embarrassed I stuffed it in my mouth and tried to focus best I could.

Before I was expecting any type of conclusion it was over and I was overcome with emotion. I teared up trying to see through the watery blur and Mel was now asking "what is it"? and my dumb brain malfunctioned causing my response, a classic to be roasted about for years, "It's... a... a baby." I like to roll out the clever one liners, but this wasn't that. Angrily, in no mood, her voice took a chilling descent "boy or girl"

She was an amazing first-time mother, the albums of pictures spelled out how much she loved that little girl and lately while transferring those photos to new albums it brought the waters back blurring my sight once more. I never knew but she had written sweet notes on the back of many of them. Valued like finding a stash of diamonds her words never known to me are now inches away. Thank you, babe, for these secret notes, you never knew how much they would mean one day.

Her last writing, I mentioned was a letter to the Province of BC. The parking charges were being reinstated at the hospitals, since being paused when covid began, and she wanted to advocate on behalf of the nurses seeing that they were going to have to pay once again sending many of them walking long distances before being on their feet all day caring for the many like her.

I took the time to type out her letter, and I noticed how she was struggling with her words and articulation more at this point. Her meds and the brain tumors were posing a true roadblock to her passion for writing and expressing her heart for others, but she did keep fighting in her own way and it boasts of her true character. At the time, some of the Canadian truckers had been holding rallies at government buildings and sadly this included hospitals. The covid restrictions tying the protest to medical establishments.

The protest she was referring to had taken place at St Paul's Hospital in February. I can remember walking down the crowded sidewalk of protestors trying to focus on Melanie and her needs. I had gone to pick up her favorite desserts from a bakery down the road, my mind still reeling from the sad news I had been told an hour earlier.

Horns honking and yelling seemed so out of place, we had just been told that her cancer had spread to her brain and was inoperable. My thoughts were spiraling while my heartrate rose and I lost it, yelling at a man in a pickup "Stop honking, my wife is in this hospital with brain cancer." His eyes got big as he promptly rolled up his window, his horn silenced out of many. I walked the hallway near the ER observing medical workers entering after being yelled at and even roughed up by the people outside, one worker holding his head saying he had been struck. "How is this sanity" I thought to myself.

I cringed as nurses told me they had to walk through those crowds and were told by administrators not to wear scrubs while outside. One protestor was so worked up he had a heart attack and found himself in a stretcher being cared for by the very people he opposed.

I know there are many opinions out there and I respect everyone's basis for them. I only want to address how the behavior from some had sadly affected innocent workers trying to care for many in their moment of need including my wife. I'm hoping we're past all this, and we can start to come together as a people.

(Her letter)

Dear Editor.

As a current patient at a hospital and a recent patient of both VGH and St. Paul's Hospital I believe whole heartedly that our nurses and doctors need to have their parking paid simply as part of compensation for the job they do.

I have watched nurses with tears rolling down their cheeks as they were denigrated and abused by redneck people pretending to be truck drivers as they spat on and swore at the men and women that were fighting to save lives. At minimum their parking should be covered simply because they save our lives daily.

I get there are logistics with lack of room, but nurses and doctors should come first, then patients and partners of patients. Visitors to short term patients should pay as it isn't really a hardship for short term.

When the weather is nice parking at the church (in Abby) is a great option but to arrive at work at 6/7 am soaking wet arriving to start a shift is just not cool.

In short, there's absolutely no reason parking should not be included in their job. When nurses & doctors are treating heart attack patients that are attacking them outside the hospital and treating them with undeserved courtesy & kindness and having to walk blocks away to their cars to avoid paying fees, is not cool. Nothing is cool about preparing to come to work.

Please Bonnie Henry, we know you have a lot on your plate, but please support these that have supported us throughout the pandemic also daily in our fights to live.

-Melanie

Yesterday I watched as one more memory drove away. This track car was a purchase made in uncertain times in the early months when Mel had been diagnosed. She had told me the week before to look at it. "You're an amazing husband, great Dad and you deserve something like that for a hobby" -her words. I think she was being generous, and I knew we didn't have the extra cash, so I went to the bank and put up my other ride as collateral not sure of my odds, but it worked out and only $200. a month.

We lined up a day to look at it and she met her good friend Caroline for BBQ oyster treats near my workplace in Blaine prior to the car appointment. The plan was to pick her up on my way to view the very loud muscle car. She had never tried gummies or Medical Marijuana but wanted to before starting her chemo regiment in case it would help her and she found out quickly that it wasn't for her when the effects began. It ended with her guzzling a quart of milk at a gas station, the white relief streaming down the sides of her cheeks like a scene in a train wreck comedy.

We kept the appointment at her insistence, I offered to just take her home, but she said she would wait in the car and promised to behave. That was it, I was on my own with the obvious decision, sampling the thunderous revs as it put a smile to the corner of my mouth, and her gathering one more story about how she "let me" make that purchase while she was under the influence.

The flip side of this story, a young man had his sights on this Firebird years back when a string of mechanic shops horse traded it throughout Lynden WA using it in their lots as a flagship of their talent and racing her on weekends. This now car enthusiast and experienced racer (Mick) remembered it for many years and when he saw my ad, he had to take it seriously. We talked a few times, but Mel was my top priority as her health was riding like a roller-coaster at the time, I had gone silent on him, and he lost my contact info when the ad ran out.

Recently I had a random text from him that he was in town and had actually been driving around looking for traces of this car in back yards, asking strangers, finally posting a plea to anyone knowing anything about my car. My decision, a lot easier this time resulting in a goodbye, or maybe a "see ya later" Masa AZ is a short flight to see Firebird 2.0 light up the track.

Chapter 18

Us

July 5

Today's is our 30th anniversary Melanie, my love. I know you had hopes of a large outdoor "tent revival" styled event, over 150 friends and family sharing an amazing tribute of how exceptional our love is and the renewing our vows. Food trucks and country dancing on a mountainside in Chilliwack would have been where we stood today with the many souls who have witnessed and contributed to this unique earthly experience which was "us."

Thank you for believing in me always, loving me thoroughly and blessing me with laughter, insightful conversation, your radiant presence and your simple beauty.

I'm realizing how rare our love was, I thought I understood and cherished our almost fictional storybook while you were at my side, and I rethink that daily. I miss our companionship and simply talking about our days before the darkness of night.

I used to wonder how you could listen to one Playlist for weeks and months. The same songs over and over. Your feel-good tunes were heard through the bathroom door while you soaked, outside under the shade of an umbrella or while falling asleep at night. Now I understand, I can't put those same tunes down and I don't plan to.

I told you I'll be ok, and I will. Some days I think I'll make it through without watery interruptions, but the triggers are sudden. In a strange way I welcome them, they remind me how deeply I've been infected by you, that has strong value. When tears come, they bring a warmth that starts above my brow and flows through my mind. I don't know how, but it's comforting. I fear one day it'll be less, then gone, along with that comfort.

June 30th, 1992 -We were engaged to be married, and had just gone through weeks of marriage counseling, we were definitely in love but there was the concerning fact that Mel was pregnant and 18. Pastor Mark was very thorough in bringing us through added sessions regarding our quickly coming little family. Another pastor recommended not to marry. I'd like to say we chose correctly.

I was 27, didn't have much of a bank roll and the concern of failure due to social stats was a thought I'm sure on the minds of many. What some didn't factor was a major advantage we had, God had a plan, and the major players were our own flesh and blood and of course you, our friends.

Our wedding was simple yet beautiful, low budget but very special. From the cake which took a hard bump in transit and was mended by the caring hands of family, to the rained-out gardens and plan B, under last minute cover below the gift shop sign, her being the true gift.

We went through life patterned after that day. Don't ask me why but we always seemed to need that rueful revision to our plan A. Maybe that was part of what made us work together so well, we adapted to simply figuring shit out. And there was always more in that creek. Friends and family were always by our side, and I thank you.

Her mom recently told me she and her Bible study group had been praying for someone to come into Mel's life that would help her onto a good path after a relationship of abuse and some questionable friend choices. Two weeks later I walked onto the scene. All these years I thought she had saved me, but we had saved each other.

The years came and went with many hard roads but much love and laughter. I hope you all see life differently, treat others with more care, look deeper into the eyes of your lovers or look further for true love.

It's out there and we all deserve this wonderful experience.

Our vows:

I Randy, take Melanie to be my lawful wedded wife

to love you with all my heart and affection

To endow you with all my earthly possessions

To give you the honor of my name

To share with you the grace of my God

To have and to hold you from this day forward

For better or worse richer or poorer

In sickness and in health

I promise to comfort and cherish you in joy and in sorrow

And to preserve our Holy matrimony until the coming of our

Lord Jesus Christ

or until God will separate us by death

For thereto I give you my promise.

I Melanie, take you Randy to be my lawful husband

to have and to hold from this day forward.

For better or worse, richer, or poorer, in sickness and in health

To love and obey you

to honor and keep you in joy and in sorrow

And to preserve this bond wholly and unbroken

until the coming of our lord

Jesus Christ or until God by death will separate us.

For thereto I give you my promise, where you go, I will go

Where you watch I will watch

Your people shall be my people

And your God shall be my God.

These rings are emblems of purity and endless devotion.

They show how lasting and imperishable we are to each other.

This is the part where we would have had our bride and groom dance to Shania Twains -You're still the one, and Mel would have proudly kicked up her heel to reveal her pink rhinestone cowboy boots she was so proud of.

Chapter 19

Alone, in Appearance

July 16

Chase is doing well; he had a review with his oncologist yesterday and all the outcomes were favorable. His swelling in his neck is gone, his PET scan showed expected bone marrow activity with this diagnosis which will continue to be fought while continuing the treatments. His attitude amazes me, always positive much like how his mama was. I'll continue posting his progress throughout the rest of the year.

Twelve weeks has come and gone, I decided to follow up and read through it realizing to myself, man, I got pretty chatty.

I don't know what happens now. Thoughts of travel writing is an interest, If not just the occasional trip. My future involves water since I sold my race car and bought a small live aboard sailboat. Taking it to Cali, storing it there flying in for winter getaways another thought.

Life without Melanie isn't my choice. For now, I choose "with her" in this new form. I still talk to her, I'm sure this is normal right? She still surprises me with the odd coincidence, that must be her. She actually told me to get out and go to a concert the other day in a way that had to be from her spirit form. I bought two tickets to Kenny Chesney in Seattle, I'm sending this post from our seats, alone in appearance but she'll be beside me. It just feels right to do it this way at this point. Her words stay with me in the form of a bracelet I had engraved, her last valentines note. I never was symbolic this way, now I give myself permission.

I'm really torn with what to do with this social presence I created. It was never meant to be indefinite, but it has worth noting the followers, "you" being the value.

July 19

Our morning coffee was preferred fresh ground, usually enjoyed under covers to keep things warm and close. We had this wedding gift three decades ago, a Braun grinder which still works today amazingly. The yellowed plastic started chafing so electrical tape was a "temporary" solution. The side and lid melted slightly from its neighboring stove & fry pan. The base broken away from two taps a day freeing the precious granules.

This small appliance became symbolic one day when we both looked at it realizing it was the last of the hard-working wedding gifts from so long ago. This prize not worthy of a yard sale had renewed value. Retired, not thrown but tucked away, we revered the relic having little to do with its purpose, rather endurance. No words were said but a long meaningful embrace as we understood the message presented to us.

My apartment lays packed away in storage, unit 22 holds the modern sleek grinder purchased recently with intent for the next long term. It sits safely in a box under a box among many so I un-retire the relic from the back of the cupboard here at home. Today my coffee will have a memorable taste unique only to me.

I hope you all have a symbolic item, a card, or a trinket that's a reminder of longevity, trust, caring and sacrifice. There may be damage, repair may be far too obvious, and it may not seem to work. Remember endurance has it's worth and remember the deserved long embrace.

Let us not lose heart in doing good, for in due time we will reap if we do not grow weary.

-Galatians 6:9

July 29

I never analyzed our wedding video this much before. I notice small nuances I hadn't seen. When she put the ring on my finger, she had an uncontainable smile as she raised her eyes. I know that smile from the rest, gleeful, all the stress of having a wedding gone, all the uncertainty whether this was the right path or not, also, gone.

I know I'm not the only one affected by this loss, you are all with me. She was special and her infectious laugh wasn't the only thing about her that drew us in.

We'll prop each other up best we can, hope for lighter sweeter days reminding ourselves just how precious the ones around us are.

Aug 5

Chase is doing exceptional with his chemo. He had the results of a PET scan yesterday and the tumors in his lymph nodes are reduced to half, right on schedule! Thanks for all the prayers and love sent his way. He is halfway through his treatments and rock-starring it all the way.

I had assembled a photo book I made when the kids were younger, when we took them for their first trip to Disney Land and Universal Studios. The theme even back then, and as far as I can remember was "Love", what Mel was all about.

Chapter 20

The Cabin

Aug 6

"The Shack" is a movie we watched while I was visiting Mel at "The Cabin", a place she had rented up on the side of a mountain in Chilliwack. March 2021, she just had her reversal surgery freeing her from the ileostomy bag which she had for almost a year. It was traumatic at times getting her system to work again requiring minimal steps to the bathroom which the small cabin provided.

One of the pilots through her work (Terry) had arranged this place of healing for her also bringing two more lovely people into her orbit Brian and Carol the gracious landlords turned close friends.

The Cabin was a place where Mel had time for silence. We shared many close moments with an amazing view of Cultus Lake, cupped beautifully between the distant mountains, too far for a typical lake view, but real enough, beckoning one to dip a finger down through the clouds touching the water's surface like God would do.

During the throws of covid, and all the political unrest, this peaceful perch was perfect for healing thoughts and focusing on us. She did however spend an adequate amount of the time nested there alone when I was working, I sensed she needed the alone time. Thoughts of her mortality were close by, for all of us, how could they not be.

Weekends and the ability for me to work remotely gave us more when we needed it, but she also wanted me to keep a balance of time with our home life and the kids.

The campfire, porch swing and the ultra-comfortable king bed gave the cabin the 5 stars she needed, although the bear visit could have been omitted and thankfully was uneventful.

Living a short walk up the trail Carol would visit her from time to time bearing the gift of a book and bottle of favored wine, they would sit around the campfire, I hadn't had the pleasure of joining them for their chats, but I can guarantee there was laughter and a tear or two as they solved life's traumas and shared the joys. That simple cabin magnetized many loved friends, close ones would even fly in joining her glorious earthy spot and simply enjoy her radiance. Kath, her sister who she relied on daily would do anything and did much, "extra" always. Those two were the closest of sisters, I know she misses her much like I do.

111

The simplest things are sometimes the best. This campfire, a bit of an awkward slope made with not quite enough big rocks in a humble circle made it both adequate and perfect, the point being the flames and the eye getting lost in them. My thoughts of improving the setting were resigned to introspection and heartfelt conversation followed by long stretches of silence. This was what we needed in a world full of unrest.

Those months are a treasure tucked back in my mind now, I can see possibilities opening for new beauty hoping this dirt path I'm on now broadens to a luscious meadow where I can once again imagine God's finger dipping through the clouds.

The "Shack" (the movie) I would highly recommend. Unknowingly I used one of the theme songs in the slide show at her memorial "Phone Call to God" the movie itself deals with how we can trust him when it seems so unfair that we have lost so much.

April 28th, two days before she passed away, I was sitting in Whitespot Restaurant finishing my meal after taking a break from her bedside. We had sat for many family meals here when the kids were little usually with the Dueck clan, pirate packs, the boat-shaped and colorful cardboard creations proudly showcased before their little blonde heads contained a bounty of gold chocolate coins, fries, a burger and a milkshake. Usually, a highchair on one or two ends' scraps scattered around the floor calling for an extra tip.

It was hard to believe I was here now, in this moment. I knew she was leaving me soon, I "wished it" at this point knowing she wouldn't want this, her still slow state prolonged, no longer communicative, her sweet smiles enduring the pain, gone. This was it, the transition for her to the stars and mine to an uncertain future as a lone soul.

It caught my eye, a sailboat cruising around the corner at eye level as the server hurried it past me. "It's still a thing" I thought to myself with a smile. She leaned forward presenting the pirate pack to a little girl and plates to her family, an older sister, and average looking parents who I had noticed were engaged with them laughing and talking, I also noticed cellphones weren't present, a rule Mel had made for our table even at home.

I was swarming with emotion as I asked my server for my check and theirs too. As I walked out, I thought to myself "they'll never know why some stranger paid their tab," but I knew and that's all that mattered. You never know how one action you take could affect anther's future. Those parents may have gone through their own struggles that day with a new outlook and a different outcome. In another realm, I believe Mel was there as a "quiet force" compelling me.

Looking through the stories Mel had started to write I realized, these must be shared. Partially done, but her story, her words which she poured a piece of herself into. I need to help her complete these best I can. She had the university degree but I'm here now, gifted only with time and a hope that I can do her justice. I'm once again compelled by the "quiet force" to do this rather than seeing them eventually lost. I once heard some motivational advice, "if you can, you must", and I will.

In a new way Melanie, the author and me, her co-author will be doing something together that is meaningful, once again a team, and this warms my heart.

I had ordered some pens to organize my financial files, the silver fine point sharpies had a nice feel to them, and I found myself practicing and refining my signature, pages later I noticed I had used up a section of the spiral notebook, I also realized I would need to practice for the books I now plan to sign for our readers one day soon, with a hint of Mel in this new artform.

There will be two books for now, first my memoir "Twelve Loving Weeks" and another the cancer journal she started which I haven't named yet. These hopes are giving me new energy right now as well as purpose, and a sense that "all is well."

Chapter 21

Pain's Absence

August 21

The waves kissed the hull of the MacGregor 26M as it began cruising across Harrison Lake. This boat frequented my saved photos clipped from the many web searches I had done over the years. I had imagined it to be ours for the last two decades, we never had the extra to afford the moderate motor/sailor, now I was making a new start with an old dream.

Mel at my side was the plan, her loose bangs being wisped by the gentle lake breeze as she would cast her proud smile at me accompanied by the dimple I loved so much. Now her spirit form is beckoned. This boat, originally named Phantom was to become "SS Mello" yet to be applied to the port and starboard sides.

The day had been hot, and the wind was perfect. Alone for my debut voyage was my choice if she couldn't accompany me, it just felt right. I hadn't sailed since I was a teen and decided to just motor around getting used to the boat and its secrets. I had planned to stay overnight, sleeping in the more than generous cabin but cruising around the shoreline I realized I had chosen a lake with little to no places to anchor.

With options diminishing, I surveyed the sheer cliffs cutting the water's edge and dismissed ideas of tying off to unstable logs crutched between rocks and the mysterious darkness below the surface.

I was running out of daylight. I had already called the marina and no luck; they didn't welcome overnights. Finally, there it was, a tiny cove with a private beach I could rest the stern on giving us, me and the boat, a bed of sand for the night.

It was perfect. I could have made a campfire on the sand, could have watched the sunset, made an exquisite meal, my feeling was of amazement, but an emptiness lingered. I wasn't supposed to be here alone, and it was all wrong. So, I bedded down resting my head to her favorite playlist one more time drifting away with a hope of joining her in a dream.

The morning brought curiosity when I woke to complete silence. The gentle gurgles and splashes of the night were gone, my fuzzy waking brain confused, there had to be some water play.

Tiny eyes of the small birds crouched in the tree's watched and chirped as the hatch slid open, the messy haired creature emerged from the thing intruding their paradise. I looked out at the morning mist forming from the still watery surface making its journey to the clouds for the endless cycle, the lake was like an immense sheet of glass. The scene brought a notable feeling of calm. I knew she was there, the stillness of that morning to represent her pain's absence, her being at peace.

My tears are less frequent, I can talk about her without a quiver in my voice, but a new event has emerged, sobs wake me at night without the recall of a dream. Perhaps a reminder that I'm still rebuilding my still fragile heart.

September 1

Dad jokes crossed over the flames near missing the browning marshmallows being crafted over the propane campfire. Camping at Cultus Lake was exactly what my heart needed, spending a casual weekend with my cousins and their families. The humor was as refreshing as the air flowing through the tall cedars.

The last joke of the night was unintentional while trying to coordinate with Lynette, the sausages I had brought for breakfast the next morning. "You save your sausages for the boys at home" she said noting she had bacon instead.

"I'd rather use up the sausages, how about I save your bacon"

There it was. Chuckles followed with surprised looks as the organic punchline surfaced.

The weekend provided one more stitch closer to a mended heart. The paddle boarding, beachside visits and parting hugs were the comfort and support I needed.

The dream I had on the last night was of humor, I remember doing a stand-up routine which is too weird to go into, but I will note I had to turn away from the crowd due to my uncontainable laughter I had. The nights following and to this day I no longer wake with sobs. Someone's prayers were answered. Probably my parents. Thanks Mom & Dad

On my road back home, I was one in an audience witnessing a beautiful rainbow. I stopped on the quiet farm road to capture it when my phone dings with a text from Lynette sharing the same rainbow from their perspective further up the Fraser Valley. I'll take it as Mel saying "I was there with you all, as I am now.

Chase is doing well with his treatments and we're thankful for the experience modern medicine has given, combined with all the well wishes and prayers you are providing. We realized after his two nights camping; how valuable his rest is. Although his treatments seem uneventful, we still must guard him and stay alert to his needs.

Chapter 22

Rays of Warmth

September 29

Nothing could replace our fondest Oregon trip made 26 years ago but we had to try one more time this weekend. Mel and I often reminisced about that first trip, although she had traveled to much more exotic destinations since. That simple tent nestled in a low dip of sand among the Lyme Grass and Sea Spurge, only steps from the ocean. Our youngest at the time, Austin, bashful as he posed for the picture while the salty breeze played with his white-blonde hair, and Savannah, toting her pink bucket filled with seashells and driftwood carefully selected by an artful eye.

We made the road trip a ritual every other year lately, trying to supersede the memory but knowing it was meant to be respected not bettered, its purpose reminding us of simplicity.

We had returned often with Colby and Chase, more adventurous types, involving surf boards and quads with much laughter and tales of adventure told on the ride out of the dunes.

I spent a considerable amount of time just sitting on the beach this time, analyzing the light of the sun as it bounced and flickered off only a select few waves, at a perfect angle to guide the flashes to my line of sight. Those moments and reflections were only for me, a direct communication from the sun and the great expanse of its home. I longed for a connection to her, and this would have to be it. The rays of warmth and the dreams I'm still having at night, comforting me that she's still somewhere, still real.

I've talked about her chattiness and how I miss it, I also now realize my dependency for her to start a dialog when we were with friends, she broke the ice, usually adding the pieces to mixed drinks. She was the master of conversation, now I must retrain my mind to take the lead. It was natural for her, but she would push me to engage after she got things rolling and I did, usually surprising myself.

Autumn brings forgotten colors and renewed landscapes as our blanket of green fades. Christmas is next, this will be hard. I can try to be positive, keep moving forward, but the truth that she won't be with us is in our path.

Five months have passed, it feels like an eternity. I'm so glad I have the kids and they have me.

Chase has three more treatments left and all seems well. The chemo is starting to build in his system giving him reactions which he can counter with meds. His positive and cheerful attitude amazes me every day. Puppy therapy has been key to his recovery, and good for us all.

Thank you for your prayers, everyone.

Chapter 23

Recovery

October 17

Reflecting on her last month, days, hours are hard to relive in my mind, but it is part of the process. The tears still come but farther apart, when they come, they're welcome knowing that my heart is still there, she's still there.

I feel like I'm wandering lately even though I'm home, I try to keep busy, loose myself in a project, distraction helps but I still miss my friend, her gentle voice, her laughter, her way of changing my mood from gloom to brightness.

When I venture out, I feel different when I'm among people. I look into the eyes of clerks and strangers I pass thinking to myself "you have no idea what I've experienced, the valuable gift you have and don't know until its missing." I used to be one of them, doing the daily grind not truly appreciating the fact that I was loved by someone absent for eight hours and would reunite for what was actually important.

Disclosing her passing with people I meet is done with hesitation. When I do, the conversation goes solemn, and the mood is stifled and unretrievable. It's not their fault, but not mine either. I'm resigned to silence avoiding the awkward moment.

My experience these past six months has been traumatic in many ways, I watched my pretty wife change physical form due to the steroids and various other drugs. Seeing her in constant discomfort and anxiousness was so hard to watch, but better than seeing her arch her back writhing in pain as I had seen months before.

Her last few days haunt me. She breathed with longer gaps, when she spoke it was hard for her to annunciate since her mouth was dry, which must have really pissed her off. She was used to being so articulate, so animated with crafted words.

One morning I noticed dried paths of tears fanned out on her temples revealed by the morning sun. She had cried during the night trapped in her semi-paralyzed state and I hadn't been there for her even though I was beside her all night. She must have been awake, unable to relay her desperation.

My comfort for her was constant all our marriage as hers was for me. There were many times I needed her emotional support after a hard day at work. Being a manager sounds important, and I prided myself on always finding a common ground or a solution, but the mental toll is taxing, when workers unload all their stresses on you, or upper management dictates seemingly impossible demands. She was there always, giving comfort in my moments of desperation. I remember how I had gone to talk to her manager at one point when she was a gate agent in Abbotsford, stating how she was being treated unfairly and was being misunderstood, and she had done the same for me at my job a few years back, I was recently told.

We were each other's advocate in so many ways. I often wondered why couples and families are required to give the best of themselves at their jobs and the worn-out remainder of our day to each other. It's also comforting to remember how we relied on each other, propping each other up when we were down. It seemed like we were never emotionally drained at the same time, like God knew the balance we needed.

We were slipping apart now. It saddens me that I couldn't hold her hand through the night as she slept, floating at her side as she wanders in her dream world or especially when she entered into eternity. We all must do this one thing alone, no matter how rich or significant we are on this earth, all our accomplishments are left behind and our true character, our spirit, is all we take into the next life.

The tiny sponge rigged to a suction pump on the wall was no longer an option for her relief now. I had been taught to use it to keep her mouth hydrated at the very least, the suction designed to pull back the spray of water only moistening her mouth but not passing to her throat. When I gave it to her, she would close her mouth trying to savor all she could.

She asked me for water begging, "I'll pay anything," she pleaded like she had a desperate addiction, "Rand… I want just three bowls of water." Later "a bucket."

The nurse explained to me, her inability to swallow meant fluids would pool in her lungs where there was already the constant gurgle as she breathed. The sound was uncomfortable only to the ones listening. When she did have a choking fit it was jarring. I never experienced terror like that, the nurses were very responsive with tubing and drugs to settle my sweet wife.

As her healthcare advocate, I was burdened with the decision to take her off antibiotics first, then stopping her IV fluids since they did the same as her getting sponge water. It was "less cruel" to simply starve her body until it resigned.

I see the stages of death differently now. I never understood how someone could say they didn't want treatment, facing a formidable foe as this. I was proud to do battle at her side. We were teammates through the good times and bad. Money struggles, failed ventures even bankruptcy, our marriage survived some major challenges. This was more like a war in comparison, and I am proud that we held true to each other until the very end.

While editing this book, I printed a random page to view the positioning on paper and as I held it in my hand, I realized, this was the first printed form of TLW. The first page, my first book ever!

Like a businessman framing his first dollar, I had to preserve this moment, probably only important to me.

I then noticed the page I chose was "Chapter 13", usually a reference to bankruptcy, depletion and failure but also a form of new beginning, recourse, and a start to recovery. I also noted the heading "A Lot of Information" I chuckled to myself, alone in the room, "it's perfect" I said out loud.

It was hard to do at times, a lot of "coming back later" was a remedy getting me through, along with much encouragement from you.

My main reward from writing all this has been the healing. Processing such a loss could have gone in many other directions. I might have benefited by going for counselling at times, and there may be a day where I choose to, there was also a day I would have found solace in a bottle, thank God I've been spared this addiction. For your comfort and my own, I write. *Words* being my medicine.

I'm so happy that many of you have been helped. Some of you were so close to Mel, others had a view into who she was and I hope you found inspiration. I've said how Mel was all about love and inclusion but with that comes hope.

Hope is the beginning of a plan. It may be simply spreading a smile wherever you go, to empower and encourage others. Whatever happens in your daily struggle is meant to be in some way, good or bad, the important thing is movement, always leading to a result. If the result is bad, much like bankruptcy, the positive you must take from that is *knowledge and correction* which results in *hope*.

For the last few months, I noticed if I didn't post every two weeks, around the 1st and the 15th, I was notified there were new views on TLW, sometimes over twenty in one day, prodding me to share another entry, more of our story. It was comforting, knowing there were more of you out there that were finding comfort where I did. You gave me courage to keep going, sharing, giving more, and receiving more.

When I was 14 years old, I had a bad accident involving a golf club, my head, and a stay in the hospital with complete loss of speech due to the impact just above my left ear, apparently where words are formed. I could make sentences in my mind; I knew what I was meaning to say but it was coming out as babble.

I remember the worried looks of family and friends as they came to visit, and I spoke gibberish. Their eyes showed fear as I attempted a conversation, but for some reason I felt peace knowing I was going to be ok.

The doctor reassured us that most likely the brain would remember the needed function, swelling would reduce, and I would speak normally again. It took about a month, and I was saying sentences, longer words took more time.

The brain is an amazing part of our being. It holds our key to living an amazing life, or one of sorrow and hardship. That 14-year-old boy today, is articulating hope and comfort to many. I'm glad I could help you while it helped me.

After this memoir is published, I'll be working on her/our book, it's already in progress, she actually started it in 2019 right after her diagnosis. It's more of a story, a novel, and I'm excited to write with her. Melanie's paragraphs and sentences merged with mine. Some of you will also recognize parts taken from her Facebook, her posts, her enjoyable words, and fun spirit with us again.

I'm sending out a big "Thank you" to everyone. Your warm caring hearts are so valued. Melanie's memories and mine have been greatly honored. You've helped me through this, the hardest challenge in my life. I'm left with a desire to continue what she was so good at, helping others and spreading sunshine. I Love you all so very much.

In everything you do

everyone you face

every day

Lead with Love

-Rand

I love you all beyond a shadow of a doubt

and I want you to remember...

Love will heal anything

and it's all that matters

at the end of the day.

Raise a glass for the rest of the season.

Love Mel

139

Manufactured by Amazon.ca
Bolton, ON

30040213R00081